The Machinery of Life

by

Darren J Beaney

First published 2021 by The Hedgehog Poetry Press

Published in the UK by
The Hedgehog Poetry Press
5, Coppack House
Churchill Avenue
Clevedon
BS21 6QW

www.hedgehogpress.co.uk

ISBN: 978-1-913499-37-2

Copyright © Darren J Beaney 2021

Cover design by Matt Bemment

The right of Darren J Beaney to be identified as the author of this work has been asserted in accordance with the Copyright, Designs and Patents Act 1988.

All rights reserved. No part of this publication may be reproduced, stored in or introduced into a retrieval system, or transmitted in any form, or by any means (electronic, mechanical, photocopying, recording or otherwise) without prior written permissions of the publisher. Any person who does any unauthorised act in relation to this publication may be liable for criminal prosecution and civil claims for damages.

9 8 7 6 5 4 3 2 1

A CIP Catalogue record for this book is available from the British Library.

For Jo,

Once again -

with gusto

xxx

Contents

What is love?	7
Blocked heart	8
Twister	9
Your heart out	10
Disturbance	11
The sound of recovery	12
Together we feel the melody	13
Ask and you shall see	14
What's love got to do with it?	15
The occasional revamp keeps us engrossed	16
Love you tender	17
Eros in East Preston	18
I thought he was Cupid	20
Strung out and under the influence	21
Ask the boffins, dreamers, historians & the poets	22
Under this poem	24
Strewn	25
Postcard perfect	26
Love at first light	27
True lust	28
Love	29
Love is...	30
How many times can I say it?	32

WHAT IS LOVE?

It is documented.
Musty, weathered. Ancient sentiment,
essence so deep. Bursting with a concoction
of meaning, the nitty gritty of which hides
in a labyrinth.
Yet it   breaks out   in perpetuum,
vibrant and animated.   It pedals round

the earth preying on the blushing. Crafty cat
burglar stealing hearts for pure pleasure. Silent
assailant plundering and destroying. You may
stare it in the face for an age before finally
putting 1 + 1 together.   I remember
sighting it, in a flash, a dayglo acidic angel
dancing on bubbles.   It feeds simply off three little words

that may shoot effortlessly from the lip, sprayed
with the ease of spittle or a teasing hint.
Where does that simple lyric go when uttered,
to the land of meaningless tosh, to live short
and die with stale gossip, or flourish
sustaining lifelong work, lasting, bequeathed as a coffin companion.

Some live by the sound of those words, contracted
to their harmony. Others flaunt them
like over inflated cash, buying worthless passion. Love
creates jesters, sultans and migrants.
Decodes high times and mockery.
It is who we are, with or without it.

I will be spot-on to its proposition.

BLOCKED HEART

Sunday afternoon sessions
spent settling into sagging skin.
Drinking non-stop philosophy. Pint glass
tunnel vision, black light
dregs. Forecast low, no claims required.

Sentiment on the juke box, ghosts
in each lyric. Eros at the bar
starts a commotion. In a heartbeat
I know a quaint cottage view,
orchard sky, virtual daybreak.

You let Eros buy you a pint.
Down it at first sight. Give me one
of your hi-fi smiles, and shout *"Read the signs,
punk"*. You order tequila with a splash.
My insides start to undulate, the ripples
move in reverse, meet in the middle.

I put in a call to *Dynorod*
   for my heart.

TWISTER

                When our paths
                                        thwacked
                                                      into one
                                        another
I tumbled. Consumed by a tornado
                    like Dorothy
                                          I found myself
                              swept along
              to an alternate place.

              I caught myself pondering...

      I must be brainless
nothing makes sense

    and

       if only I could locate my heart,
              but you whipped it away

                and

I wish I had the courage to take you by the hand,
       drag you home.
                    You gleamed

bright like rubies and emeralds
       glinting in the glory of a straw-hat morning.
          I was your pretty. Love developed,
          everything became clear.
                Blemish and edit.
                Black and white.
         You and me.
                Polychromatic.

YOUR HEART OUT

I am shanty boy
                     prising
your heart from its shell with black
and blue sea salt kisses and vigorous
vinegar-stained handshakes.
Anticipating my underarm clout
will lead to a persuasive getaway,
as I jemmy your heart out.   Convincingly

plunging through the fresh skimpy
glory hole before absconding.
I will substitute Cupids' quivering
arrows with harpoons of circumstance.
Enact repeated romantic episodes of fondness,
retell my tenderness for you, until
I shoot your heart out.   When I win my prize

I will be a wild saint.
Tempt you with this tasty project, as I fall
for your full-frontal tease. We will collapse,
a couple of gasping creatures,
you holding your heart out,
me embracing it

       assured with easy balance.

DISTURBANCE

I saw you.
A scenario for disruption.
Your glide
       through space
                around you.

Changing
the shape of our scenery,
particles shifting
                deconstructed by your incidence.

I saw
a supernova.
Your energy
       a torrent across time
                professing to be endless.

I see us.
Our commotion
            a medley
                    as we venture
                          as one.

THE SOUND OF RECOVERY

she generates a fracas

a roar of static
as enthused as an overworked Geiger counter

triggers a riot

she is my saving grace

listen
I am in recovery

TOGETHER WE FEEL THE MELODY

Ours is sentimental dialect,
close whispers translate into industrial language
of survival.

Settling in for evening bugle call.
You regard what I utter,
add daylight to what I say.

We wax lyrical, enthusiasm profound.
Our chorus continues to chime.
We are number one, our serenade virtuoso.

Our performance takes centre stage.
We rock our love
bandstand.

ASK AND YOU SHALL SEE

Why do I wear glasses?
Why was I late to the party?
Why were we drunk?
            But our eyes collided
in an imprecise instant:
            now our love is visible

across landmasses,
no exaggeration required.

WHAT'S LOVE GOT TO DO WITH IT?

Love has everything to do with us.
As I step over your piles of derelict clothes and wonder...
    When you abandon a sorry looking
tea bag on the side, never mind
the stains.   As I snuffle.
   When I perform
like a draining squirt or regular stand up.

The times I just.... Well   just don't....

On occasions.   When we are both pissed.   Those days
it is all down to me, certainly not you.   When I forget sweet, running
on empty. How about when you just don't make sense.
   When we cry.   When our hold is like *Locktite*.
As the morning peeps and amazes us,
evenings as we sink into comfort, one.

Hearing each other, telling it like it is after we neglect.
When you are there and I am somewhere else.
   When you are happy, and always
when you are at ease!

THE OCCASIONAL REVAMP KEEPS US ENGROSSED

Every now & again
we shuffle our front.
 Treasure a new vantage point
for holistic smudging.   Somewhere
cosier for our two-seater.
 (A misplaced pouf
wants to be side-stepped
or suffer stubbed reproach).   The odd
reorder of composed paper
gives us something to discuss.   Declutter.

Meaningful colour our decoration.
 We avoid walls,
go for exposed & fascinating.
 Equalise, even if it means a reshuffle
of the ruddy
drinks cabinet.   Private members
chamber arranged equally,
no side holds majority.
       Room   to   flow
    full force
of the right feng.

LOVE YOU TENDER

Over time
I seem to have lost my gentle
touch.

Middle age spread has left me heavy handed.
I fumble
about your person all fingers,
thumbs and knuckles,
as delicate as a rocket launch.

                Making you tremble
at the thought
of what is to come.

I grope my way around you
like an awful puppeteer.
My gangling hands run amuck on your body, gallop
over you like a rotund shire horse.
Yet, eventually you succumb,
submit to my awkward wrestler's hold
and become damp
putty in my sweaty mitts. I am not sure why,
since - I can seldom put my awkward
finger on it.

EROS IN EAST PRESTON

Hotshot talent
wasted.   Gut reactions
fragments of archaeology.
His fable binds,   unbinds,   dangles
by a fleece.   He curses Apollo for leaving
him suburban and wonders
why?

       Hung up on deficient tall tales.   Time
to skedaddle.   He scatters
his essence.   Congeals as out of sync archive.   Soon
a tourist, assuming the name Cupid,
his preferred waggery.   Secures lodgings
at The Sea View Inn,
overlooking shaggy dog parlour.

 In Tudor Rose he enumerates
orders in antique Greek.   Barmaid
attends, he recounts midsummer mischief.
Egyptian queen & Roman soldier.
  Hotheads in Verona.   Darts
cast oblivious, arrow tips misaligned.
Tales of truth frayed.   Lies and brutality,

                                      the war
in his helix.

Tipsy,   feeling metaxu,   Eros hunts. Something
of an odyssey here. Settles for sweet and sour
chicken balls served exclusive of sacrifice.
        Surfeit.   Epic.   Settling
on shingle under cryptic clouds
and heroic semi-circle moon.

He cites Socrates' marvellous
lunacy. Plato's disdain. He acts
out his famous Sappho tease and replays
missing the target with Foucault.   Spatters
at Uranus "what was the fucking deal
          with Nietzsche?"

Back in his room he listens to Littlehampton
Friday night sirens.   Lays on ancient divan, his noodle
like an illuminated globe.
 Casts spinning thoughts way back
to his parents. Relives the contours of their love
the ultimate in pleasure and pain.

He embraces his own spun-out anti-climax.
 Nothing alters.
 He lives his own
                    impossible binding.

I THOUGHT HE WAS CUPID

When Ares and Aphrodite played gods
of infidelity,
frontlines slept;
archers dreamed.
Only air died.

Begot
........Eros,
................blackballed Olympian,
wanting mythology.

Buoyant hybrid dynamo, whirling band
of colour.   Master of disguise. Cherished
circus performer, high on Piccadilly
and shady idolatry.   To this day he bootlegs
his way skirting Atlas's assumptions.

STRUNG OUT AND UNDER THE INFLUENCE

We are Sid & Nancy,
loaded and spent.
Cameos in a Cheech & Chong flick.

We are habit.
Beyond recreational.
Strung out on infinite street corners.

I am hooked
on your joints.
Ache for your tang, that smack.

I crank you up.
You trip my dragon.
Spin under my skin.

I dilate for you.
Up all night.
Persist through your veins,   rave in our hearts.

Our score is high.
Aphrodite is our dealer.
            Only losers waste love.

ASK THE BOFFINS, DREAMERS, HISTORIANS & THE POETS

Scientists tried
to let it flourish
in dishy mould. Got in a whirl
experimenting with DNA.
Found the true elements, but not the exact mix.
Distilled it, diluted data. Got lost in taxonomy.
Discovered it has to be the real thing,
cannot be replicated
and shyly published their findings
without conclusion.

The philosophers gathered
and chatted each other up,
ignoring Abelard. Plato held a symposium.
Engels looked backwards.
They took a long hard Roschian look
at their hearts, supposed something seminal.
Grand statements proclaimed,
eternal models offered, still
to be fully understood.

The historians
inferred love by numbers.
Exhumed early signs. New kingdom
love notes, damage smitten by ego.
Located myrtles in the foam
but excavated Psyche.
Recorded 999 ships for Helen.
Traced Napoleonic foreign affairs back to Hippolyte. Found proof
of fairy tale romance.

The poets
tried.   Penned flowers. Dickered cliché
for metaphor. Flapped angst
touching images of lust.
Cried with joy. Celebrated love lost.
Composing ever after.   Here we go again.

UNDER THIS POEM

I sleep warm in words and after
thoughts. I plunge oneiric. Dreams hurtle
uninhibited, like an excursion
of excited witty travellers.

Under this poem
I bury fears in closed casket.
Pressed into the nooks of a gothic crypt,
constructed with bottomless lines.
Unworthy of remembrance. Little more
than a set of second-string considerations.

Under this poem
you will find a peepshow to my heart,
discover my soul.
You will not see coincidence.

STREWN

Each night love folds me away.   Neat.
I sleep in Odysseus's bed and fall
through Penelope's dropped stitches.
Dreams are virtuous and eternal.   Cosy,
intricate.

                                        Morning at first sight

is   slow-mo. I wake like a hesitant
Polaroid. Instinct flexuous, on the rise.
My bunk head gaze rotates over you
and notices.   Last night love

scattered you about the room.   Untidy.
You erect me topsy turvy. I can't straighten
you out.   It's alternative attraction,
living normal chaos.

        It's love.

POSTCARD PERFECT

You promenade beside the ocean.   I balance
   on a seawall, view a picture
      postcard perfect.   You   saunter across the beach,
         walk my way.   I want to be the warm sun
on your bronze shoulders.
    I imagine myself nonchalant breeze,
a satisfied sigh on your blushed cheek.
     I wish to be the yielding sand
under your feet. And I long to be the trillions
   of tiny grains between your toes
       that you cannot help but take home.

LOVE AT FIRST LIGHT

At a flicker before daybreak
I unsteadily scramble from sleep.   Toss away
compact covers: they feel way too abrupt.

Bones bewildered by nightmares
feel a long time away,
far from curated.   I yawn, stretch,
win the struggle, take the glory.   Avoid

my morning tipping.   Leisurely limbs unearth
some elasticity. Perhaps later
they will know some bounce.
A fractured whimper escapes my lips,
hounded by spit eternal.   I instigate a cockcrow

train of thought and it dawns on me that I remain
unburied.   I gaze at you as you stir.
    Your fuss warms
my cockles, rouses shifty passion.

              I incline.   You squeeze.   We nestle
                                        secure.

TRUE LUST

A droplet of lover's sweat
explodes on my chest
spreads
like quicksilver
slinking
larva warmth
stealing
toward the valley
above my belly.   And comes
to rest
suitably
over my heart.   And melts
into pores.
Itches through dermis
swirls
its way
into vena cava.
Shifts
direction.   And mutates.

Her
speck
of passion.

LOVE

        Is it really
just a four-letter word.

        Is it not
a kebab stick stuffed with emotion.
Hunger, verging on cannibalistic.
A recipe with basic
ingredients.

        It is sacrifice.
Worship. Fundamental.
Blasphemous.
Followed by devout, spurned by agnostic.
Plagued with unheard prayers.

        It is ambivalent.
Imagined or for real. A caress.
Often forgotten, misplaced.
Some do it by rote.
A kiss.

        Is it constructed.
A maze with euphoria
at its heart. The hook
of Sixties pop. Unbelievably wet
windswept moors and feisty girls.
You can read all about it.

        It may
have reason.
There is a rhyme. Perhaps
universal. Tricky.
It might be them, I am adamant
it is us. But without you, I swear
it has no meaning.

LOVE IS...

At first sight
its guise is somewhat scary.   Sheepishly
we approach, daring to flirt with danger.
We submit, take a flutter.   Faster.

    Don't stop.
Belly churning.
Blood curdling enthusiasm jammed deep in our throats.
Trapped shrieks tasting of anticipation and fairground grease.

                  Cyclonic eyeballs
                                swivel.
            Vision blurs
                with amber fog.
                            hang on
        tight – enjoy the thrill.
                                    Twists
                                        &
                                    turns.
                                        Cork
                        screws.

.kcab-hctiwS   'suoisɹǝʌuI

Creeping up impossibly steep gradients. Eventually,
            briefly ᵦ a l a n c e ᵈ.   On top of the world
                    ready to

                                p
                                l
                                u   Ninety-nine miles
                                m   a second
                                m   into oblivion.
                                e   All lights spell **L.O.V.E**
                                t

Feelings x x xcelerate. Eager to be petrified.
Rushing to free butterflies & dragonflies.
Together we touch the sky. Wave hands in the air.
Undulate as one. Embrace.
Our vertigo develops slow motion lovesick.

Share the pleasure of duet screams.
Palms clammier. Clutching harder. Knuckles popping. Catch
a shared sharp intake of sweet breath.
Shout above the roar, laugh.
Promise
never spare the queasy. Keep our convulsions.

HOW MANY TIMES CAN I SAY IT?

   Stuck on an extra-long solo venture
                              alternating opposing opinions
              stay in my silo versus hanging out in cattle markets

until I heard your music   I interrupted
   your singing
            "is your halo velvet"
   you put down your cello vexed   slowly
      removed pink silk gloves   face full of smirk
my heart pumped blood
            through jello veins
I quaked in a voice reserved
   for gods   yes   Apollo verbals.
            "hello Venus"
I thundered   my voice amplified   roaring in a speeding
              tremolo vehicle
  my confidence increased
     jam-packed with desire   I sputtered
   the full weight of my kilo verse

you flounced over
   gliding as if in a pedalo vessel
   gave me the once over
            a gigolo vetted   you grinned
  my head span   we embraced
a clincher   we dated   frequented
         finest bordello venues
drank cheap wine   ate exotic food
           tomatillo vegan stew
  we swapped tokens   you bought
        me a polo vest   I knitted you an itchy
        wool pullover   we leapt
now   I am evolving
        a pig in clover

ACKNOWLEDGEMENTS

What is love was previously published by City Limits Publishing in *Through Loving Words volume 2.*

A version of Postcard Perfect was previously published by The Hedgehog Poetry Press in *Wishing You Were There*

A version of Love is... was previously published by City Limits Publishing in *Through Loving Words volume 1.*

BIG THANKS TO:

John McCullough - some of the poems in this pamphlet were written for my MA Creative Writing dissertation for which John provided great supervision, advice and feedback

The participants in my research for my dissertation, in particular Matt Bemment - cheers for your insights mate and thanks again for a super cover design

and

Adam Majsai - for providing the inspiration for the poem that sits on page 30 of this pamphlet, thanks my old friend

Alan Meggs - my MA buddy and critical friend for reading the poems

Barbara - my MA buddy, critical friend and fellow dragonfly for reading these poems again and again and again and again...

Mark Hedgehog - for the vison that is The Hedgehog Poetry Press and for taking another punt on my words

Everyone who has ever attended Flight of the Dragonfly - inspirations all

My family - love you all x

Eros - for finding me

and finally, of course, Jo xxx

DJB May 2021